my itty-bitty bio

Tiera Fletc

Published in the United States of America by Cherry Lake Publishing
Ann Arbor, Michigan
www.cherrylakepublishing.com

Content Adviser: Jessica Criales, Doctoral Candidate, History Department, Rutgers University
Reading Adviser: Marla Conn MS, Ed., Literacy specialist, Read-Ability, Inc.
Book Design: Jennifer Wahl
Illustrator: Jeff Bane

Photo Credits: ©ESB Professional/Shutterstock, 5; ©Adisa/Shutterstock, 7; ©Monkey Business Images/Shutterstock, 9; ©Jaromir Chalabala/Shutterstock, 11, 22; © Courtesy of Fletcher Family, 13, 17, 21, 23; ©Marcio Jose Bastos Silva/Shutterstock, 15; ©Alones/Shutterstock, 19; Cover, 6, 8, 16, Jeff Bane; Various frames throughout, ©Shutterstock Images

Library of Congress Cataloging-in-Publication Data

Names: Spiller, Sara, author.
Title: Tiera Fletcher / Sara Spiller.
Description: Ann Arbor : Cherry Lake Publishing, 2018. | Series: My itty-bitty bio | Includes bibliographical references and index.
Identifiers: LCCN 2018003108| ISBN 9781534128811 (hardcover) | ISBN 9781534132016 (pbk.) | ISBN 9781534130517 (pdf) | ISBN 9781534133716 (hosted ebook)
Subjects: LCSH: Fletcher, Tiera, 1995---Juvenile literature. | Women aerospace engineers--United States--Biography--Juvenile literature.
Classification: LCC TL789.85.F54 S65 2018 | DDC 629.1092 [B] --dc23
LC record available at https://lccn.loc.gov/2018003108

Printed in the United States of America
Corporate Graphics

table of contents

About the author: Sara Spiller is a native of the state of Michigan. She enjoys reading comic books and hanging out with her cats. She wants to help empower people all over the world, including women engineers.

About the illustrator: Jeff Bane and his two business partners own a studio along the American River in Folsom, California, home of the 1849 Gold Rush. When Jeff's not sketching or illustrating for clients, he's either swimming or kayaking in the river to relax.

my story

I was born in Georgia in 1995.
I have a brother and a sister.

Our parents helped us learn.

I helped my mother go shopping.
I added up the total.

My father taught me how to **measure** objects.

I played four musical **instruments**. I counted the **notes**.

Music and math aren't so different!

I wanted to be an **aerospace engineer**. I was 11 years old.

My family helped me.

What do you want to be when you're older?

Later, I chose a special school. I traveled far to get there.

I was in many **honor societies**.

I went to the Massachusetts Institute of Technology. This school trains engineers.

Where would you like to go to school?

I got a job at The Boeing Company. It makes aircraft.

I worked with **NASA**. It sends people to space.

I worked on NASA's Space Launch System.

It is the strongest rocket in history. It will take humans to **Mars**.

I follow my dreams. My future is bright.

I want others to believe in themselves too!

What would you like to ask me?

timeline

2006

1990

Born
1995

2017

2095

glossary

aerospace engineer (AIR-oh-spase en-juh-NEER) someone who is trained to draw plans for and build machines having to do with flying or space travel

honor societies (AH-nur suh-SYE-ih-teez) groups for students who do very well in school

instruments (IN-struh-muhnts) objects used to make music

Mars (MAHRZ) the fourth planet away from the sun, between Earth and Jupiter

measure (MEZH-ur) to find out the size or weight of something

NASA (NASS-uh) the National Aeronautics and Space Administration; it is in charge of the United States' space program

notes (NOTES) musical sounds, or the symbols for musical sounds

index